WORLD ALMANAC® LIBRARY OF THE MIDDLE AGES

travel and trade

IN THE MIDDLE AGES

FIONA MACDONALD

Gareth Stevens
Publishing

Please visit our web site at: www.garethstevens.com
For a free color catalog describing our list of high-quality books,
call 1-800-542-2595 (USA) or 1-800-387-3178 (Canada).
Gareth Stevens Publishing's fax: 1-877-542-2596.

Library of Congress Cataloging-in-Publication Data

Macdonald, Fiona.
    Travel and trade in the Middle Ages / by Fiona Macdonald.
        p. cm. — (World Almanac Library of the Middle Ages)
    Includes bibliographical references and index.
    ISBN-10: 0-8368-5899-9 (lib. bdg.)
    ISBN-10: 0-8368-5908-1 (softcover)
    1. Travel, Medieval—Juvenile literature.   2. Commerce—History—
Medieval, 500–1500—Juvenile literature.   I. Title.   Series.
    G369.M33   2005
    914.04'1—dc22
                                        2005043261

First published in 2006 by
World Almanac® Library
An Imprint of Gareth Stevens Publishing
1 Reader's Digest Road
Pleasantville, NY 10570-7000 USA

Copyright © 2006 by World Almanac® Library.

Produced by White-Thomson Publishing Ltd.
Editor: Walter Kossmann
Designer: Malcolm Walker
Photo researcher: Amy Sparks
World Almanac® Library editorial direction: Valerie J. Weber
World Almanac® Library editor: Jenette Donovan Guntly
World Almanac® Library art direction: Tammy West
World Almanac® Library graphic design: Kami Koenig
World Almanac® Library production: Jessica Morris and Robert Kraus

Photo credits:
Akg-Images: pp. cover and 33 (Staatsarchiv, Hamburg), 4 (British Library), 5, 9, 41 (Bibliothèque Nationale,
Paris), 8 (Erich Lessing), 12 (Heritage), 13 (Akg-Images), 19 (VISIOARS), 25 (Andrea Jemolo), 26 (Joseph
Martin), 29 (Museo di Capodimonte, Naples/Dagli Orti), 38 (Jean-Louis Nou); Art Archive:
pp. 7 (Travelsite/Colasanti), 10 (Bibliothèque Municipale, Valenciennes/Dagli Orti), 18 (Dagli Orti), 20 (Museo
Correr, Venice/Dagli Orti), 43 (top) (Marine Museum, Lisbon/Dagli Orti); Bridgeman Art Library: pp. 11 (British
Library), 15 (Musée Conde, Chantilly, Giraudon), 16 (Palazzo Medici-Riccardi, Florence), 22, 35 (Bibliothèque
Nationale, Paris), 30 (Museo Civico, Bologna/Roger-Viollet), 31 (Bibliothèque Municipale, Rouen/Giraudon), 36
(Archivio di Stato, Siena), 37 (Musées Royaux des Beaux-Arts de Belgique, Brussels/Giraudon); Corbis: p. 34;
Topfoto: pp. title page and 23, 43 (bottom) (British Library); Werner Forman: pp. 42, 40.

Cover: A colored miniature shows fifteenth-century Hamburg, a harbor city in the Hanseatic League.
Title page: Both ocean-going ships and smaller boats are shown in this painting of Venice's harbor in about 1340.

Printed in the United States of America

3 4 5 6 7 8 9 09 08

Contents

Words that appear in the glossary are printed in **boldface** type the first time they occur in the text.

Source References on page 45 give bibliographic information on quoted material. See numbers ([1]) at the bottom of quotations for their source numbers.

The Middle Ages are the period between ancient and early modern times—the years from about A.D. 500 to 1500. In that time, Europe changed dramatically. The Middle Ages began with the collapse of the **Roman Empire** and with "**barbarian**" tribes invading from the north and east. In the early years of the Middle Ages, western European farmers struggled to survive. This period ended with European merchants eagerly seeking new international markets, European travelers looking for fresh lands and continents unknown to them to explore, European artists creating revolutionary new styles, and European thinkers putting forward powerful new ideas in religion, government, and philosophy.

What Were the "Middle Ages" Like?

Some people view the period as the "Dark Ages," an era marked by ignorance and brutality. It is true that **medieval** people faced difficult lives marred by hard work, deadly diseases, and dreadful wars, but their lives included more than that.

The Middle Ages were also a time of growing population, developing technology, increasing trade, and fresh ideas. New villages and towns were built; new fields were cleared; and, with the help of new tools like the wheeled iron plow, farms produced more food. **Caravans** brought silks and spices from faraway lands in Asia. New sports and games, such as soccer, golf, chess, and playing cards, became popular. Musicians, singers, acrobats, and dancers entertained crowds at fairs and festivals. Traveling troupes performed plays that mixed humor with moral messages for anyone who would stop and listen.

A HISTORIAN'S VIEW

"A hundred years ago the medieval centuries . . . were widely regarded as 'The Dark Ages.' . . . It was an age whose art was barbaric or 'Gothic'— a millennium of darkness—a thousand years without a bath. Today . . . scholarship [has] demonstrated clearly that the medieval period was an epoch of immense vitality and profound creativity."
C. Warren Hollister [1]

Religion, education, and government all changed. Christianity spread throughout Europe and became more powerful. Another major faith—Islam—was born and carried into Europe from the Middle East. New schools and universities trained young men as scholars or for careers in the Church, medicine, and the law. Medieval rulers, judges, and ordinary citizens

◀ Wealthy travelers enjoy a meal in a richly decorated chamber, probably a private dining room at an inn. This image was painted around 1450 to illustrate a handwritten manuscript copy of *The Travels of Sir John Mandeville*, a collection of exciting travel adventure stories mixing fact and fiction.

▲ Marco Polo (lived 1254–1324) was the most famous traveler to live in medieval times. He spent almost twenty-two years traveling through Asia, trading and working for the Mongol emperor of China, Kublai Khan. He is shown in this fourteenth-century picture leaving his home city of Venice, Italy, together with his uncles, merchants Niccolo and Maffeo Polo.

created **parliaments**, jury trials, and the common law. These changes in the fabric of society still shape our world today.

Historians divide the entire period into two parts. In the early Middle Ages, from about A.D. 500 to 1000, Europe adjusted to the changes caused by the fall of the Roman Empire and the formation of new kingdoms by Germanic peoples. In these years, the Christian Church took form and Europeans withstood new invasions. In the late Middle Ages, from about 1000 to 1500, medieval life and culture matured. This period saw population growth and economic expansion, the rise of towns and universities, the building of great cathedrals and mosques, and the launching of the **Crusades**.

Risky and Exciting

Both travel and trade are ancient human activities. Over many centuries, they have helped communities develop, change, unite, quarrel, or simply survive. They have allowed individual men and women to learn new skills, meet new people, experience adventure, gain knowledge, and satisfy personal curiosity. They have helped some people grow very rich and led to others becoming poor, enslaved, or exploited. They have been risky, exhausting, and exciting.

Throughout the Middle Ages, people had many different reasons for travel. They set out to find food, seek raw materials, get rare and valuable treasures, show religious devotion, study, take part in politics, or make war. Most medieval people traded crops they had grown or things they had made for items they could not produce themselves or for money. Some medieval men— and a few women—made a living just by buying and selling. Others provided services, such as money changing or banking, that made traders' lives much easier.

Very often during the medieval centuries, travel and trade were combined. Trade provided a reason for travel—and the profits to pay for it. Many of the world's most important roads and seaways were created and used by traders.

Trade was also the reason why many late medieval travelers set out on daring journeys to explore the world. The facts they discovered, the sights they saw, and the people they met changed human lives forever. These medieval explorers created a new era in human history.

CHAPTER 1

Europe's Land and People

edieval Europe was a divided continent. Its land and peoples were separated by geography, history, climate, and politics into many different regions, peoples, and loyalties. In addition, since the people came from various ethnic backgrounds, such as Latin ones in southern Europe and Germanic and Scandinavian ones in northern Europe, they developed a variety of languages.

Mountains, Rivers, and Seas

Geographically, northern and western Europe was cut off from southern and eastern Europe by two great mountain ranges, the Alps (between France, Germany, and Italy) and the Pyrenees (between France and Spain). More mountains—the Balkans and the Carpathians—divided northern and western Europe from Asia and the lands bordering the eastern Mediterranean Sea. These mountains were all so high that their upper slopes were covered year round with snow and ice. Only a few steep, dangerous passes (narrow ways through high mountains) allowed people to travel through them on foot, which they did mostly in summertime.

Lowland regions in Europe were divided by mighty rivers: principally the Rhine, the Rhone, and the Danube. These were so wide that, for most of their length, medieval people could not build bridges to span them, and they were so deep or fast-flowing that only expert ferrymen would dare to row across them.

Around the coast of Europe, thousands of islands were separate from the mainland. Some, such as Britain and Ireland, were large and close to Europe's landmass. Others, such as the Faeroes (in the North Atlantic Ocean) were tiny and far out at sea. All these islands depended on ships crossing stormy waters to make contact with the rest of Europe. They also relied on the sea as a means of protection.

Ways of Surviving

Medieval Europe also had a very varied climate, which ranged from ice and snow in Scandinavia

Saint Bernard
(c. A.D. 996–1081)

Bernard, a Frenchman, was a Christian monk who lived in the Alps, close to high, dangerous mountain passes. As an act of charity, he set up two hospices (shelters) where exhausted travelers could find shelter. With his fellow monks, he trained big, strong dogs to find travelers lost in the snow and lead the lost people to safety. Today, the Saint Bernard dog breed is still named after him.

to hot, semi-desert conditions in southern Spain. To provide food, farmers, hunters, and gatherers needed local knowledge of crops, animals, soils, wild produce—and the weather. These many contrasting environments meant that European peoples had to follow different lifestyles in order to survive.

In cold mountain regions, medieval farmers raised goats and cattle for meat and milk and grew hardy grains, such as rye. In warmer lowland regions with rich soils, they grew wheat, beans, and many different vegetables. They planted orchards for fresh fruit and vines to grow grapes for wine. If medieval families lived by the sea, they went fishing or collected shellfish and seaweed or made salt (essential for preserving medieval foods). If they lived close to forests, they gathered wild berries, nuts, and mushrooms. If medieval people's crops failed, or they failed to find wild food, they went hungry and sometimes died. Few had spare money to spend on luxuries.

▲ The jagged peak of Mont Blanc (White Mountain), 15,800-feet (4,814-meters) high, towers above the Alps, Europe's highest mountain range. Medieval travelers from present-day France and Germany had to cross the Alps to travel south or face a long, dangerous journey by sea.

Local Produce on Sale in Dublin, Ireland, 1233

- Wheat
- Oats
- Oxen
- Horses
- Cows
- Pigs
- Sheep
- Hides (cattle skins)
- Wool
- Salt
- Lard
- Cheese
- Butter
- Honey
- Herring
- Salmon

Extracted by author from a list of taxes collected at Dublin

Divided Peoples

Politically, Europe was divided throughout the Middle Ages. The peoples of Europe were also divided. They spoke many different languages, observed many different customs, and were governed by different laws. Like languages, some legal systems were based on Roman traditions, some were introduced by invaders, and others had ancient local origins. Throughout the Middle Ages, these were amended by local rulers who added many new laws. They were also strongly influenced by Christian religious ideas.

At the start of the Middle Ages, most Europeans were **pagans**. They worshiped local tribal gods or nature spirits that lived in woods and water. In A.D. 324, however, Christianity became the official religion of the Roman Empire, and from then on, the Christian Church sent missionaries to convert pagan communities. Some medieval rulers forced people they conquered to accept Christianity. Banning old religions helped strengthen the new rulers' political control.

LANGUAGE BARRIERS

Some medieval European languages, such as Italian, Spanish, and French, developed from Latin spoken by peoples of the old Roman Empire. Others, such as German, Russian, and Gaelic or Breton (spoken by **Celtic** peoples in present-day Scotland, Ireland, and Brittany in France) were based on languages used by European peoples before the Romans became powerful. Some languages, such as Hungarian and Turkish, were introduced by invaders.

All European languages changed and developed over the medieval centuries. Most were written down then for the first time. Sometimes they blended together to create a new language, such as English, which is derived from elements of German, French, Danish, and Celtic.

▼ The stave church (a church made of wooden poles and planks) at Urnes, Norway, was built about 1100, barely one hundred years after Norway and neighboring Scandinavian kingdoms had been converted to Christianity.

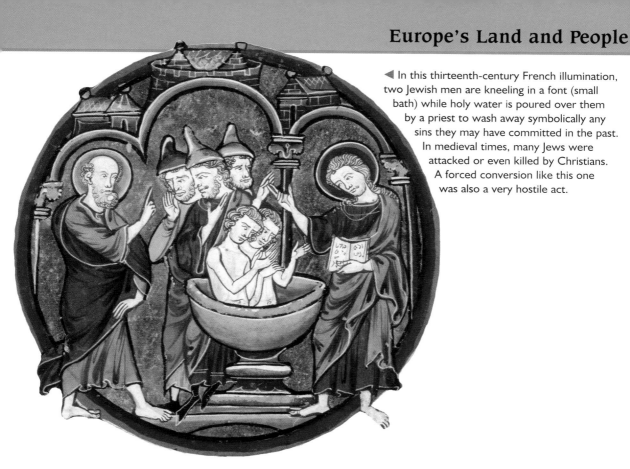

In this thirteenth-century French illumination, two Jewish men are kneeling in a font (small bath) while holy water is poured over them by a priest to wash away symbolically any sins they may have committed in the past. In medieval times, many Jews were attacked or even killed by Christians. A forced conversion like this one was also a very hostile act.

By 1500, most Europeans were Christians. In western Europe, they belonged to the Catholic Church, based in Rome. In eastern Europe, they belonged to **Orthodox Churches** based in Constantinople and Moscow. There were quarrels between leaders of these Churches, and within each Church, as well. Religious **dissidents**, known as heretics, were often cruelly punished by rulers and Church courts for daring to disobey Church discipline.

For most of the Middle Ages, there were small communities of Jewish people in Europe. They lived and worked in trading cities in England, Italy, Spain, Germany, and France. From about A.D. 800, there were also Muslims—originally from North Africa—who arrived with conquering armies and settled in southern Spain. The last Muslim rulers were driven from Spain by Christian kings in 1492, along with most of Spain's Jews. Ordinary Spanish Muslim people were also forced to leave or give up their faith.

DESCRIPTION OF JEWISH MERCHANTS, A.D. 847

"These merchants speak Arabic, Persian, Greek, French, Spanish, and Russian. They journey from west to east, from east to west, partly by land and partly by sea."
Adapted by the author [2]

Contacts and Conflicts

All these different languages, laws, customs, and beliefs made contacts between European peoples difficult and sometimes dangerous. Misunderstandings easily led to quarrels, and quarrels soon led to wars. By the end of the Middle Ages, medieval people also felt a growing sense of national identity and pride. However, few medieval states or peoples were entirely self-sufficient or cut off from the others. Already, at the start of the Middle Ages, they had been linked by travel and trade.

travel technology

urope is a large land area covering almost 4 million square miles (10.4 million square kilometers). In medieval times, it was not an easy place to travel. In addition to geographical obstacles and cultural differences, medieval travelers also faced natural barriers, such as dark, gloomy forests inhabited by bears, wolves, and wild boar, as well as rough scrubland with wiry, prickly shoulder-high bushes. There were treacherous bogs and **quicksand**, where travelers sank and drowned, and marshland infested with biting insects. These insects carried dangerous diseases, including malaria.

Dangers of Travel

Medieval seas and coasts were often extremely dangerous, except to sailors and **pilots** with very detailed local knowledge. Even they could be fooled, though, by freak weather conditions such as a sudden storm. Medieval people also believed in a variety of monsters that lived in seas and oceans. These creatures lay in wait to attack unwary travelers.

Europe's varied, changeable climate meant that travelers had to face snow, ice, frost, or fog

HOW ENGLAND'S KING JOHN LOST HIS TREASURE IN QUICKSAND, 1216

*"Some **packhorses** and several members of the King's household were sucked into quicksand where the Well-stream meets the sea. . . . His household belongings, his holy **relics**, and other contents of his chapel were lost."*
Ralph of Coggeshall, medieval chronicler [3]

▲ Medieval sailors faced death by drowning if their boats were swamped in heavy seas or overturned by whales. These anxious mariners—and a whale larger than their vessels—were pictured in a thirteenth-century manuscript.

▲ This diagram, from a fourteenth-century collection of poems from southern France, shows the four seasons of the year. The artist has imagined them as four people, constantly turning the earth like a wheel and changing the weather.

if they set out in winter or risk searing heat, dust, and drought in summertime. Strong winds and violent storms were common in spring and autumn. Rivers and streams flooded unpredictably after heavy rain. There was no really safe time to travel, but medieval people preferred to journey in spring. The days were longer—northern Europe has more than twelve hours of darkness daily in winter—and the weather was milder.

Maps and Guides

Another important fact is that many medieval travelers did not have detailed, accurate information to help them plan their journeys and follow their chosen route. In the Middle Ages, maps were extremely rare and extraordinarily expensive. They were not designed as aids to

GOING ON A SPRING PILGRIMAGE

The start of "The Canterbury Tales" —one of the most famous medieval English poems, written around 1390—describes how fine spring weather encouraged medieval people to go on long religious **pilgrimages**:

"When April with its sweet refreshing showers
Has soaked dried-up old March right to the root
And bathed each vein with liquid that has powers
To bring life there, and fertilize the flowers.
When South Winds also have, with their
    sweet breath
Brought back to life, in every wood and heath
The tender shoots and buds—and the fresh Sun
Into the Ram* one half his course has run,
And many little birds make melody
And sleep through all the night with open eye
(For Nature urges them to have courage)
Then people long to go on pilgrimage."

*the zodiac sign of Aries
Translated by the author

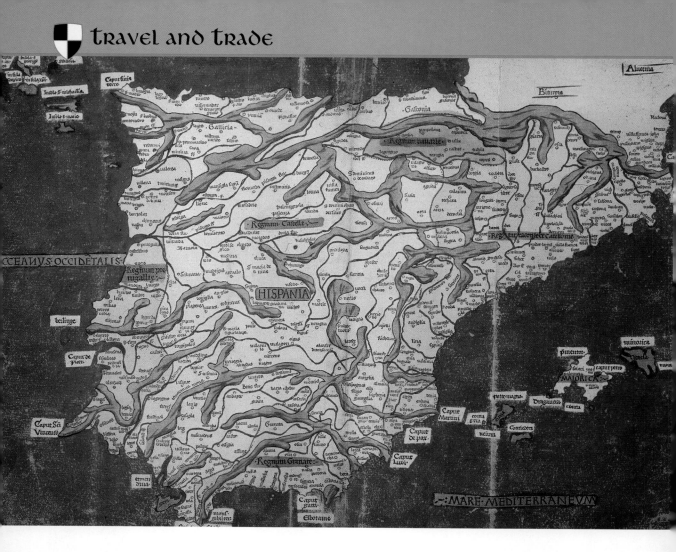

▲ Important information for travelers, including rivers (blue), mountains (brown), and dangerous rocky islands around the coast, are shown on this map of the Iberian Peninsula (today's Spain and Portugal), made by a German **cartographer** in 1482.

navigation. Mostly, they were used by scholars as a way of displaying religious ideas about the creation of the world. Only kings—and their agents—or Church scholars could afford to buy them or have them made.

Most medieval maps had little detailed practical information. They either copied ancient Greek notions of geography (for example, that there were only three continents—Europe, Asia, and Africa) or tried to convey a religious message by focusing on the holy city of Jerusalem (now divided between present-day Israel and the West Bank), in the area where Jesus Christ lived and died. Maps like these—though fascinating to medieval scholars—were of no use to the average traveler. They did not show most mountains, rivers, roads, cities, or harbors. Medieval mapmakers had no accurate way of measuring

WORLD GEOGRAPHY

*"Our ancestors . . . were of the opinion that the circle of the whole world was surrounded by . . . the Ocean on three sides. Its three parts they called Asia, Europe and Africa . . . They explain the situation of cities and palaces. . . . They locate the islands . . . among the waves. . . . But no-one has attempted to describe the impassable outer reaches of the Ocean, or has ever traveled there. . . . Because of obstructing seaweed and failing winds it is plainly **inaccessible** and unknown to anyone except God who made it."*
A medieval writer [4]

In this fifteenth-century manuscript illumination, painted in Austria, men ride on horseback and women travel in a heavy horse-drawn coach. The coachman is walking beside the horses, encouraging them to go faster by hitting them with a whip.

vast distances or showing them on the flat surfaces of maps.

At the end of the Middle Ages, large areas of Europe were still largely unexplored except by local people. They were understandably suspicious of traveling strangers who arrived from places they did not know.

Faced with difficulties of finding their way in unfamiliar territory, medieval travelers paid local guides to help them travel overland or local pilots to guide their ships close to shore. Medieval people on the move also relied on "travelers' tales" (accounts of adventurous journeys made by earlier travelers) for information about distant lands. Like many pieces of travel writing, though, these were often exaggerated to make a good story. Sometimes they were completely imaginary. The most helpful travel texts had no maps at all, but instead listed a series of landmarks with the distances between them. They instructed travelers to move from one landmark to another. That way they would be sure to reach their destination.

How Did Medieval People Travel?

Whether they were planning a long or a short journey, medieval people had only two options.

ṫravelers, Beware!

Many traditional tales tell how travelers met terrible ends in the homes of unknown strangers. For example, one ancient Scottish story describes how a younger son returned to his family home after years of hardship and danger. He was eager to share the riches won on his travels with his family but wanted to test their welcome first. He therefore asked for a night's lodgings without saying who he was. His family did not recognize him and—as they had done many times before—murdered the "stranger" to steal his belongings. It was only when, the next morning, they prepared to dispose of his dead body that they realized—to their horror—who he was.

They could travel overland: on foot, on horseback, or in carts and wagons pulled by horses, donkeys, **mules**, and oxen. Their other choice was to travel by water: across lakes, along rivers, or over the sea.

By Foot or on Horseback

Vehicles pulled by animals were extremely expensive in medieval times. (A top-quality horse could cost at least as much as a luxury car does today.) Most medieval people were poor; therefore they walked. This limited the distance they could cover every day. Usually, women and older children were expected to keep the same pace as the men.

Walkers equipped themselves for their journeys with stout leather boots, thick woolen cloaks (for warmth and to use as blankets), wide-brimmed hats (to keep off the sun and rain), and long, strong sticks called staves or staffs. These provided support when walking on rough ground and could also be used as a defensive weapon. Apart from these essentials, medieval people "traveled light," taking as little as possible with them to save energy. They carried coins in a leather or cloth purse hung from their belt or around their neck for extra security. The rest of their belongings—a water bottle, some food, and maybe a clean shirt or **chemise**—were slung in sack on their back or packed in a leather shoulder bag called a "scrip."

In contrast, rich medieval travelers could afford horses to ride. There were several different breeds. Knights and nobles rode palfreys, handsome horses with a steady gait (a horse's manner of walking), especially bred to give an easy, comfortable ride. **Squires** rode strong,

▶ These two cheerful young couples are riding on horseback for a pleasure trip in early summertime. The weather is fine, and the ground is dry, but the fifteenth-century artist who painted this manuscript illustration has still shown their road as rough and strewn with rocks and pebbles.

smart horses, called rounceys. Male servants rode hackneys—rough, cross-bred horses that were often headstrong or unreliable.

Rich noble ladies rode sidesaddle on ponies or small, gentle horses called jennets. Female servants rode pillion (astride a horse and behind a male rider). If women were old, or unwell, or pregnant, they traveled in litters (padded beds, slung on poles between two horses) or horse-drawn carriages. These litters had no springs, just a wooden seating compartment supported by wide leather straps. Litters and carriages had curtains to provide warmth and privacy and were padded with cushions for safety. Even so, they still lurched and swung most uncomfortably. It was common for passengers to get bruised and shaken on journeys across rough ground.

Death Cart

Traditionally, two-wheeled carts were used for carrying baggage—and for transporting condemned criminals to be executed by hanging. Travelers tried to avoid riding in them if possible, believing it would be unlucky. Even so, weary or wounded soldiers—and the female cooks and helpers who traveled with them—sometimes hitched lifts on two-wheeled army carts laden with tents and weapons. Exhausted workers scrambled onto farm carts at the end of a busy day in the fields.

▼ A caravan of heavily laden pack animals (camels, mules, and horses) climbs a winding pathway in the mountains of Italy around 1460. Lookouts and guards with fierce dogs walk alongside.

Most medieval carts and wagons were heavy, awkward, and slow. Their wooden wheels and iron tires were easily broken on rocky ground and quickly sank and became stuck in mud. Early medieval carts were difficult to steer. After about A.D. 800, new designs for harnesses and cart **shafts** meant that horsepower could be used more efficiently and horses guided more easily.

Horses, donkeys, and mules were also loaded with sacks, bags, or baskets and used to transport heavy loads. Many routes across medieval Europe were unsuitable for wheeled transport. A single animal carrying baggage—or a long "train" of packhorses traveling in single file—could negotiate steep mountain tracks or narrow bridges and find its way around many other obstacles.

how far, how fast?

- On an average, a man or woman walking could cover around 20 miles (32 km) a day.
- A messenger riding a fast horse could cover about 60 miles (96 km) a day.
- A two-horse baggage cart could cover about 18 miles (29 km) a day.
- A packhorse train could cover about 12 miles (19 km) a day.

Travelers and pack animals might travel farther and faster in fine weather and on smooth ground. In bad weather, or across rocky or marshy territory, they moved more slowly.

Life on the Road

Compared with today, medieval roads were few in number, far apart, and often in bad repair. Conditions were particularly bad between A.D. 500 and 800. After that time, medieval rulers tried to improve roads in their kingdoms. Following the example of Charlemagne, king of the Franks, (ruled 768–812), they paid for repairs to major roads and bridges and passed laws ordering local nobles or villagers to look after minor ones. To

ENGLISH COMPLAINTS ABOUT ROYAL GOVERNMENT

"No village or man shall be forced to build bridges at river banks, except those who ought to do so by custom and law."
Magna Carta, 1215 [5]

raise money for this, lords and other landowners charged **tolls** (taxes) to travelers passing along roads in their care.

The best medieval roads were left from Roman times. Before A.D. 500, Roman engineers and soldiers built roads right across their empire. The network ran for 53,625 miles (86,300 km)—from Scotland to Sicily and Portugal to Syria. Roman roads had cambered (slightly sloping) surfaces paved with gravel or slabs of stone and drainage ditches to catch rainfall on either side. They were as straight as practically possible, taking the shortest routes between important cities and towns. They crossed rivers and streams with well-made bridges or linked with the best ferry crossings or shallow fords.

After Roman power collapsed, medieval travelers still used these roads. The roads, however, were no longer so well maintained or carefully repaired. Slowly, Roman knowledge was lost or forgotten. Roadside ditches became blocked, and roads were flooded. Paving stones were stolen for buildings, and the roads

JOURNEY DESCRIPTION, A.D. 950

"At last, in the dark, we found the bridge leading to the town, but it was so badly broken that even local people were afraid to use it. . . . We could not find a boat, so [my companion] . . . put his shield over the holes in the bridge, and we managed to cross it safely."
Richer of Reims, a French monk [6]

themselves became overgrown by grass, bushes, and trees.

There were also many medieval roads without Roman foundations. The oldest followed pre-historic pathways—such as the "Sweet Track" in southwest England—that ran between ancient river crossings. Some medieval roads were new and led to holy sites founded by Christians and Muslims throughout the Middle Ages.

Other new roads linked trading towns, such as Norwich to London in England or Dorestad in the Netherlands, that had developed after Roman times. There were roads used by farmers and traders in lands—such as Scandinavia—where the Romans never ruled. In southern and eastern Europe, packhorse routes led to international trading ports on the shores of the Mediterranean and Black Seas.

Often, these new medieval roads were not paved. Instead, they were just wide, winding strips of land. (Historians call them "road areas.") Travelers followed their general direction, wading through mud and past puddles and potholes, hoping not to lose their way.

ROAD REPAIR IN SOUTHERN ENGLAND, 1285

"We have learned that the high [main] roads going through your town are so damaged and pitted by the heavy traffic of carts that those using them are in constant danger of being badly injured."
King Edward I to the citizens of Dunstable [7]

▼ The remains of a fine, wide road built by Roman engineers in the city of Timgad, Algeria, about A.D. 100. It is paved with solid stone slabs laid on firm foundations of sand and gravel. Few medieval roads were in such good condition.

Traveling Community

Medieval roads were often surprisingly busy. They were used by soldiers, government officials, judges, and tax collectors, rich merchants and poor peddlers (traveling traders), servants, scholars, pilgrims, preachers, wandering minstrels (musicians), actors and other entertainers, farmers carrying country produce to town markets, and fishermen bringing fish from the sea. At certain seasons of the year, such as late summer in southern Europe, travelers also met groups of migrant laborers who journeyed to find temporary work on farms and vineyards. When their task was completed, they moved on.

All these people had lawful reasons to be traveling. They were happy to greet one another when they met but were nervous about meeting other less fortunate and less trustworthy people, who also spent time on the road. These medieval "outcasts" were mostly homeless, rootless people: orphaned children, disabled men, and abandoned wives. They traveled because they had no jobs, no houses, and often no food. Many were too old, too sick, or too weak to support themselves adequately. They straggled from town to town, hoping to find work or somewhere to live and rest for a while. They survived by begging, stealing, or benefiting from the charity of kind strangers.

In wild, lonely places, travelers also risked attack from bandits and highwaymen. These dangerous criminals lay in wait in woods or behind rocks to ambush passersby and seize their horses, food, money, and sometimes even clothes. Kings, local lords, and town councils all tried hard to catch these bandits. They passed strict laws, making highway robbery punishable by death, and sent soldiers out on patrol. King Edward I of England (ruled 1272–1307) even gave orders that all trees and bushes should be cut down on either side of main roads in his kingdom so that bandits would have nowhere to hide.

A NEW ENGLISH LAW, 1166

"Inquiry shall be made throughout each county through four law-abiding men of each town, on oath that they will tell the truth, if there is any man who is accused of being a robber or a murderer or thief, or anyone who has sheltered robbers, murderers or thieves, since the lord king was crowned." [8]

◀ Solitary travelers were often at risk from gangs of highway robbers. This man has been knocked unconscious—or maybe even killed—by vicious men and women wielding sticks and stones. To avoid such dangers, medieval travelers preferred to make their journeys in large groups, protected by lookouts or bodyguards.

For protection against bandits, most medieval people liked to travel in large groups of ten or more. If they could afford it, they hired bodyguards as well.

Places to Stay

Unless medieval travelers were making only a short daytime journey, they needed to find food, drink, and a place to rest overnight. In most parts of Europe, it was not safe to wander around after dark. In addition to bandits, there were wild animals and (so medieval people said) hostile ghosts. In the countryside, farmers and shepherds who were suspicious of strangers protected themselves with big, fierce dogs. In towns, watchmen had orders to arrest anyone found outdoors at night without an obvious purpose and lock that person up in jail.

In villages, travelers sought shelter in cottages, alehouses, stables, or barns. In towns, they rented rooms at inns or lodging houses. Some religious communities of monks and nuns also offered beds and food to visitors. In Muslim eastern Europe, there were caravansaries (stopping places for merchants) with rooms and food and secure stabling for their packhorses. If travelers were far from human settlements in empty countryside, they lit fires, wrapped themselves in their cloaks, and tethered their

▼ Long-distance travelers in Asia—and their horses—stayed overnight at merchants' lodgings, called caravansaries. These contained stables, bedrooms or dormitories, secure storerooms where merchants could lock up valuable goods, and open space for lighting cooking fires. Caravansaries were surrounded by strong walls to keep out robbers and bandits.

A MONK'S JOURNEY, 950

"I had a horse to ride and a servant boy to help me. A messenger came with us. Without money or a change of clothes, I set off. . . . As soon as we entered a dark, shadowy forest, our troubles began. We took a wrong turn at a crossroads and wandered miles out of our way. . . . By late afternoon, the sky had clouded over, and it began to rain. . . . Six miles [9.5 km] from the next town, our horse collapsed and died. . . . Only those who have suffered hardships on the road will understand how serious our situation had become. . . . The servant boy fell to the ground in despair . . . we had no way of carrying our baggage . . . the rain poured down. . . . We left the boy with the baggage, warning him not to fall asleep."
Richer of Reims [9]

horses to rocks or trees. Then they took turns sleeping or staying awake and keeping lookout.

Travel by Water

Sea travel was often quicker than making a journey overland. With a good following wind or strong ocean currents, a ship could cover 60 miles (96 km) in a day. Ships were also the most economical and convenient way of carrying large, bulky loads, such as grain or stone used for building castles and churches.

By the start of the Middle Ages, there were well-established sea routes around all the coasts of Europe for traveling short distances. Drinking water, stored in wooden barrels, did not stay fresh for long on board ship, and so captains

LICENSE ISSUED BY KING JOHN OF ENGLAND, 1206

"Let it be known by all that we [King John of England] have given a license to Alexander de Wareham to export a shipload of salt from our land of England . . . to Normandy. . . . And we command that you allow him to do this freely, without stopping him in any way."
Author's translation

made regular stops at ports, if they could, for fresh water supplies. They steered from port to port using sets of written instructions, called "**portolans,**" to guide them. There were also longer distance routes across the English Channel and North Sea and in the Mediterranean. Starting in about 800, Viking explorers pioneered new routes across the Atlantic Ocean to modern-day Iceland, Greenland, and North America. Vikings also sailed across the Baltic Sea to set up trading stations in Russia and Finland. Medieval fishermen sailed long distances or were blown north and south by gales. By about 1400, they had reached rich fishing grounds off Iceland, Greenland, and maybe Newfoundland as well as the Canary Islands and the Azores.

Sea travel could also be dangerous. Shipwrecks were common, especially in wintertime and in stormy seas such as the Mediterranean. Most voyages took place in the summer, when the weather was calmer and milder. In all seasons, pirates lay in wait to capture cargo ships or boats carrying wealthy passengers. **Wreckers** lit false **beacons** to lure sailors to their deaths along wild, rocky shores so that they could steal goods washed overboard from the wrecked vessels.

Ship Technology

Medieval ships were made of wooden planks nailed to a curved framework (the "ribs"), also made of wood. Before about 1000, most ships had shallow, open hulls with planks as seats for sailors and space for storing cargo packed in barrels, sacks, or chests. After about 1200, hulls were made larger and deeper, creating more space for cargo and passengers, and covered over with wooden decks. Wooden platforms, called "castles," were added at the **prow** and the **stern**. These were used for fighting and also as lookout posts. Simple cabins were sometimes built there.

Ships were powered by men rowing or by the wind trapped in large **canvas** sails. In the early Middle Ages, many ships were equipped with

▲ Travelers onboard wooden sailing ships are shown crossing the Indian Ocean around 1400. The sailor on the ship at left is using an astrolabe to help calculate his position at sea.

both oars and sails. Later, as long voyages became more popular, they relied on sails alone. Oars were less useful in ocean waves and swells. In northern Europe and for long voyages across open sea, sails were mostly square. In south Europe, they were often lateen (triangular). **Lateen** sails made ships more maneuverable in changing winds and shallow coastal waters. Large ships often needed to be towed into port by small boats to avoid obstacles.

Ships were steered by a large oar, or rudder, at first on the right and later at the stern. Sailors used observations of the Sun, stars, waves, currents, and seabirds to steer by. They also had simple wind vanes and compasses. Toward the end of the Middle Ages, sailors making long voyages on large ships also began to use astrolabes. These navigational instruments were disks of metal with a swiveling pointer. Medieval European sailors learned about them and how to use them by copying Muslims, who had developed them from ancient Greek originals.

Astrolabes helped sailors out of sight of land measure the height of the Sun above the horizon. From this observation, they could calculate their position north or south of the Equator. Pilots, local seamen with expert knowledge, used portolans charts, which were not very precise and covered only a few areas.

LAWS OF THE PORT OF ARLES, SOUTHERN FRANCE, 1150

"If any ship is moored to a post in the river, or is sheltering . . . because of a contrary wind, then officers of those ships must send small boats with sailors to help other ships that also want to enter the river [for safety]." [10]

Inland Waterways

Rivers and lakes were also important waterways, allowing smaller ships and flat-bottomed barges to travel along them far inland. Many of Europe's most important ports, such as London, England, were beside rivers, a long way from the sea. From early medieval times, rulers made plans to create new waterway links, such as canals between rivers, across their lands.

Inland waterway travel was not always easy, however. Rivers flowed in one direction only—down to the sea. Most medieval boats did not have the power to travel against their fast-flowing waters. Sometimes, as in Austria beside the mighty Danube River, boatmen hitched horses to their ships. The horses plodded along the riverbank, slowly dragging the ships upstream.

A Rhine-Danube Canal

In 793, Charlemagne, king of the Franks and the most powerful man in Europe, ordered workmen to dig a canal in the land now known as Germany to link two great European rivers, the Rhine and the Danube. His project failed because of marshy ground and bad weather. If it had worked, ships would have been able to sail by river from the North Sea to the Black Sea. This would have been shorter, easier, and much safer than a voyage around Europe's western and southern coasts.

▼ Large ocean-going merchant ships and small rowboats used to travel on inland waters are pictured on canals in the city of Venice, Italy, about 1340. In the background are the magnificent houses and palaces belonging to rich Venetian merchants.

CHAPTER 3

Why did medieval people travel?

 edieval travelers left home for many different reasons. Most journeys were short, muddy, dusty, and unspectacular. Longer journeys were less usual, even dirtier, more risky, but often much more exciting. Compared with tourists and business travelers today, most medieval people did not travel very far or very often. Nevertheless, both medieval men and women did occasionally leave their home villages or towns.

Local Journeys

Buyers and sellers made short trips to local markets or fairs. Hunters ventured into local forests, fishermen sailed along local coasts, and farmers led cattle, sheep, and goats up to high mountain pastures in summertime. **Cattle drovers** and goose keepers walked their herds and flocks to regional markets in autumn. Laborers left cities and towns to work in the surrounding fields every day.

INSTRUCTIONS TO A FARM SERVANT IN ICELAND, c. 1200

"Your work for two seasons will be to drive home fifty sheep from pastures by the high mountain shelter, and collect firewood in summer-time."
Author's translation

Owners of cargo ships and packhorses ran regular cargo services carrying local produce along well-known local trading routes. Merchants made frequent journeys from towns out into the countryside to buy wine, grain, raw wool, and finished woven cloth.

Travels for Government

In other short, local journeys, royal judges traveled from capital cities to try criminals held waiting for them in local prisons. Ordinary people left their villages to seek justice at local or regional courts. Government couriers hurried back and forth with urgent messages from rulers

KING HENRY II OF ENGLAND (RULED 1154-1189) ON THE MOVE

"He didn't mind the discomforts of traveling, dust and mud. He was always on the move, and he traveled unbearable distances each day. His court had to struggle after him as well as it could."
Walter Map, an eyewitness [11]

to councillors, members of parliament, and other important people. Kings and princes traveled on royal **progresses**, which were journeys to impose law and order, stop local disturbances, and display their power. Noble families rode from one castle to another, taking their prized possessions with them on lumbering carts. They moved from place to place for a variety of reasons, such as holding law courts, receiving homage from tenants and subjects, administering their estates, hunting, visiting friends and relatives, or escaping from cities in hot weather.

Travels for Faith

Church officials traveled to centers of Church government, especially Rome. Monks, priests, and scholars made their way to Europe's new universities, such as those in Paris, Naples, Bologna, Oxford, and Salamanca. They aimed to study, teach, and meet other scholars from distant lands. Brave missionaries set out into dangerous pagan territory to spread their Christian faith. Many were killed and did not return.

◀ The cathedral church of Santiago (Saint James) at Compostela, in northern Spain, was one of the most important destinations for medieval pilgrims. They passed through this twelfth-century portico to pray at the tomb of Saint James, one of the first disciples (followers) of Jesus Christ.

Muslim and Christian pilgrims made long journeys to save their souls. For Muslims, visiting the holy city of Makkah (Mecca) in Arabia was one of the five essential "pillars" (practices) supporting their faith. For Christians, going on pilgrimage to a shrine (holy place), such as Canterbury in England or Santiago de Compostela in Spain, might be inspired by a wish to honor a favorite saint and to touch relics (physical remains) and objects or clothing.

PILGRIMS AT SAINT ANDREW'S SHRINE (SCOTLAND), c. 1440

"The boastful Frenchman, the war-loving Norman, the Flemish weaver, and the rough German, English . . . Dutch . . . Roman. . . . All came to lay their prayers before Saint Andrew."
Walter Bower [12]

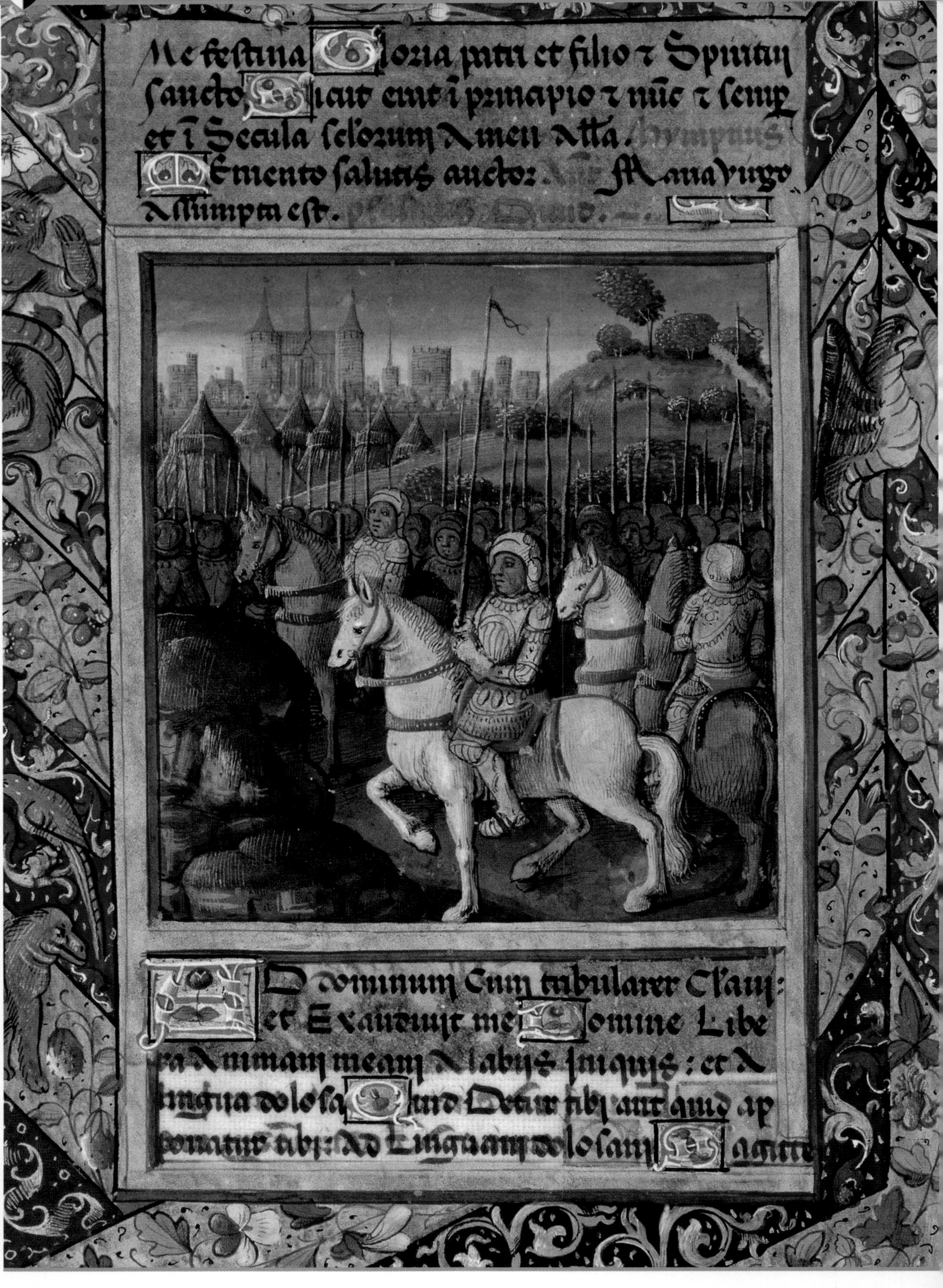

Some pilgrims were sick and traveled to shrines to pray for healing. Others wished to ask God for forgiveness or give thanks for blessings they had received. For most pilgrims, travel was an act of worship. Travel could also be an adventure, a vacation, and a chance to escape from everyday routines. Pilgrimages lasted a long time. It could take six weeks, at least, to travel between southern England and Rome.

Travels for War

Most rulers and their people wanted to increase their wealth and power. In medieval times, land ownership brought that wealth and power. Medieval armies traveled to attack, invade, conquer, and occupy. Most moved very slowly on foot. Soldiers marched in ragged lines led by knights riding on horseback. Each man carried a heavy burden of weapons, armor, and spare clothes. Troops also carried food snatched from fields and orchards in enemy territory or looted from enemy farmhouses as they moved through the countryside. Slow-moving carts and packhorses transported other equipment.

An invading army advancing through enemy territory might be on the move for months at a time. Soldiers waiting to board ships might have to wait weeks at a port. They could not leave until enough ships and crewmen had been found and the weather was calm enough for heading out to sea.

Most European wars were fought between neighboring states or by armies from powerful kingdoms invading to take over land. Two groups of medieval warriors became especially famous for long, adventurous journeys. Viking pirates sailed from Scandinavia between 800 and 1100

◀ A medieval army is on the march, as shown by a German artist in about 1490. Knights and army commanders rode on horseback. This was faster and less tiring. Their increased height above the ground also gave them an overview of their troops. Ordinary soldiers traveled on foot.

CALL FOR A CRUSADE TO THE MIDDLE EAST, 1095

"As many of you have already heard, the Turks . . . have overrun Christians living in the east. . . .They have occupied more and more land . . . and killed and captured many people. . . . They are destroying the kingdom of God. Unless you take action, they will continue to crush God's faithful people."
Pope Urban II [14]

to attack towns and villages on the coasts of Europe. From the eleventh to the fourteenth centuries, Crusaders left their homes and families and sailed or marched to the Middle East to fight for control of the Holy Land around Jerusalem.

DESCRIPTION OF A VIKING ATTACK, 845

"The Northmen [Vikings] with a hundred ships sailed up the River Seine [in France]. . . . After devastating first one river bank, then the other, they arrived in Paris without anyone fighting against them."
A monk eyewitness [13]

Migrants and Settlers

In the early Middle Ages, large numbers of people left their homes in one part of Europe to settle in another. Some moved to escape attack, such as the Franks (who went to present-day France from Germany) or the Angles and Saxons (who migrated to England from Denmark and Germany). Some traveled in search of new farmland, such as North African Muslim farmers who settled in southern Spain. Some migrated to escape the rule of strong kings, such as the Vikings who founded new colonies in Iceland and Greenland.

Travel for Trade

There were long-established networks of trading routes linking different regions of Europe. The most important ran north to south from the port of Bruges in Belgium through Paris to central France. Here it divided. One branch led south to the busy port of Marseilles (France) on the coast of the Mediterranean. The other led southeast across the Alps to Italy's most important ports, Venice and Genoa. East-west trade routes led from Prague (Czech Republic) through Switzerland and Germany to great trading cities, such as Cologne (now Köln in Germany) beside the Rhine River, then on to the North Sea.

ROYAL PROTECTION FOR MERCHANTS IN 796

Charlemagne, king of the Franks (in France), writes to Offa, king of the Mercians (in England):
"You have written to us about merchants, and by our mandate we allow they shall have protection and support in our kingdom lawfully, according to the ancient custom of trading." [15]

In far northern Europe, merchants traveled by land and sea from England, Scotland, and Germany to Poland, Russia, Scandinavia, and the **Baltic region**. From about 900 to 1100, the Rus (Vikings living in Russia) traded with the **Byzantine Empire** merchants by traveling southeast overland and then along rivers, such as the Dnieper and the Dniester, to the Black Sea.

Trade routes lasted so long because they were useful. They linked the many different peoples of Europe and allowed them to exchange the special produce of their own region to make a profit and get items they needed.

Goods that were fairly common in one country became rarities by the time they had reached another hundreds of miles away. For example, Arctic-fox furs from Scandinavia were highly valued in southern Spain. In the same way, soft, smooth Spanish leather or sumptuous velvets woven in Italy were prized by rich customers in the north. Many places were famous for workers with special skills. Weavers in Belgium and the Netherlands produced superfine linens made from flax and wonderful **tapestries**. German craftspeople made fine glassware and metalwork.

Some regions of Europe were famous for raw materials. Tin came from southwest England and coal from the northeast. Silver—used for coins, dishes, weapons, and jewelry—was mined in Germany. The best wool cloth came from England and southern Spain. Scandinavia exported timber, **pitch**, **amber**, wax, and whalebone. Other regions received money for food and drink. The Netherlands exported cod and herring; French wine was sought after throughout Europe.

All these goods, and many more, were transported by merchants who traveled all over Europe, both on land and by sea. Some only dealt in produce from their home countries; others were international traders, handling goods from many European regions as well as distant lands. Merchants' lives were extremely interesting, but they could be difficult and dangerous. Kings offered them protection because trade made countries richer. When kings or peoples quarreled, however, traveling merchants became easy targets to attack.

MERCHANTS IN DANGER, 1242

"As . . . autumn approached, the French king . . . gave orders to arrest English merchants who were traveling with their goods to sell throughout his kingdom. . . . News of this dishonorable and cruel act soon reached the king of England. To retaliate, he gave orders that French traders in England should also be arrested." [16]

▶ Big, ocean-going cargo vessels with lowered sails are tied up at well-built stone quays in the busy port of Naples, in southern Italy, pictured in the fifteenth century. Smaller ships, called "galleys," are anchored close by. Powered by oars and sails, the galleys were used to travel in the sheltered Mediterranean Sea. The harbor is guarded by a splendid castle (*left*) and strong walls with tall towers.

CHAPTER 4

Markets and Merchants

 edieval people had a choice of shopping locations. They might go to a market, visit a fair, or call at a craft workshop or merchant's warehouse. At all of them, they had the chance to obtain goods that were not available in their own small villages.

Places to Trade

At first, markets were held at places where people naturally met together, such as crossroads, bridges, and harbors. By about A.D. 1000, many of these meeting places had developed into towns. Markets were held in them once or twice a week, all year round. Town market traders sold everyday goods, such as fish, fruits and vegetables, eggs, cheese, and honey as well as an early version of take-out foods, such as hot meat pies. They also sold useful items that ordinary families could not make

for themselves, such as iron knives, leather boots, and pottery dishes.

A few traders sold farm livestock: chickens, pigs, or horses. Others sold slaves. In the early Middle Ages, slavery was common in many European lands. Then the Church forbade the

▼ A customer tries on a coat (*back*); a tailor measures cloth (*front left*), and a merchant sells fur-trimmed robes (*right*) in the covered market of Bologna in Italy, about 1350. Stacks of animal skins (*front*) are for sale.

SELLING A MUSLIM SLAVE IN SOUTHERN FRANCE, c. 1250

"We, William Alegnan and Bernard Mute, have together sold to you, John son of Peter Aleman, honestly and without deception, a certain Saracen [Muslim] slave of ours, called Aissa, for a price of nine and three-quarter pounds." [17]

...se of Christian people as slaves, but slavery continued in southern and eastern Europe, where traders sold Middle Eastern and African people to Christian families.

Many towns had a marketplace with stalls where traders displayed goods for sale. In large towns, markets might be covered by a wide roof, which sheltered traders from rain or sun. The wealthiest cities, such as Bruges (now in Belgium) had grand trading halls where brokers (dealers buying from and selling to traders) and merchants could examine valuable goods in safe, comfortable surroundings.

Fairs were very different. They were special occasions, held only once or twice a year. Most were linked to religious festivals dedicated to a Christian saint. They were holy days (holidays) when people did not have to work but could relax and enjoy themselves. Wandering minstrels, acrobats, jugglers, performing animals, and lively religious processions all added to the fun. Large fairs—for example, in the Champagne region of northern France—became important centers of international trade.

Fairs were sometimes held on open ground close to a town. This provided space for traveling merchants to pitch their tents, **graze** their pack animals, and set up their stalls. Other popular fairs, such as Saint Bartholomew's in London or Saint Ives in eastern England, were located in churchyards or other open spaces within strong, secure town walls. This also made it easier to collect profitable tolls and taxes from the fair's traders. Goods on sale at fairs included food, clothes, shoes, soap, basketwork, and costly perfumes and spices imported from distant lands. Each fair lasted for around a week, and then it was time for traders to pack up their goods and move on.

Markets and fairs were policed by officials who checked weights and measures and punished traders who sold rotten produce. Government tax collectors also levied tolls and duties from buyers and sellers.

SALISBURY, ENGLAND, MARKET COURT RULINGS, c. 1300

"*John Penrose sold unsound and unwholesome red wine. He was condemned to drink some of the wine, and have the rest poured over his head. John Russell sold 37 pigeons, all bad. He had to stand in the **pillory** while the pigeons were burned underneath.*" [18]

Markets and fairs were so profitable that medieval rulers founded new ones, or agreed to protect existing ones, in return for a share of the profits. Many of Europe's greatest medieval cities were founded as trading centers, for example, Norwich in England and Dublin in Ireland. The largest trading city was Paris in France. It had

more than 200,000 citizens in 1300. In northern Europe, rich trading towns around the Baltic Sea formed themselves into the powerful Hanseatic League to promote trade and protect shipping.

Towns were different from the surrounding countryside. They were noisier, dirtier, and much less healthy. The people who lived there were different as well. Some were extremely rich, while others were very poor. Many made their living from trade.

There were rich merchant "princes" (as proud and wealthy as any nobleman), skilled craftspeople, innkeepers, market traders, brewers, bakers, bathhouse keepers, prostitutes, and well-educated professionals, such as bankers, money changers, pharmacists, doctors, lawyers, and scribes.

There were also large numbers of poor people in most towns. They arrived seeking work and lodgings. Some did find casual employment and a miserable room to share, but others had to beg, or they would starve. Most did not survive for long after they arrived. Disease rapidly spread through dark, smelly town backstreets without drains. There was also little clean drinking water, which usually came from wells or streams and was not disinfected or purified. Rivers with towns along them were especially polluted and dangerous to drink from or even wash in.

A NEW FAIR IN LONDON, 1248

"*The king then declared that . . . he had set up a new fair at Westminster, to continue for a whole fortnight [two weeks]. At the same time, he banned similar fairs in England, and all other normal trade in London, so that more people would go to his new fair, and there would be more goods on sale there. But all the merchants who offered goods for sale suffered miserably. They had only canvas tents for shelter, and got cold and wet because of . . . bad weather. . . . They were hungry and thirsty, their feet were covered in mud, and their goods rotted in the rain.*"
Translation by author.

the hanseatic league

In 1241, a group of north European towns and cities joined together in a league (association) to protect and promote trade. Founder members were Cologne (Köln), Hamburg, and Lubeck; they were later joined by Danzig (now Gdansk, in Poland), Bremen, and around one hundred other ports and trading centers. Members of the league traded mainly in wool, cloth, linen, and silver. By the end of the Middle Ages, the league was so rich and powerful that it had its own army and navy and played an important part in politics.

Living in Towns

Better-off town families, such as craftspeople and successful traders, lived in tall, narrow houses alongside busy shopping streets. Their homes were also their place of work; many had **shutters** over front windows that they let down to form a shop counter, facing the street, with workshops and storage sheds at the back. They hung brightly painted shop signs outside their homes advertising goods for sale.

The wealthiest families—including leading merchants—lived in fine, stone palaces, with grand reception rooms and showrooms where they could display choice items for sale and welcome rich customers. They also owned huge warehouses close to busy roads or docks. They had offices known as "counting houses," where they kept detailed records of their business deals and carefully stored their money.

Coinage and Banking

For most of the Middle Ages, trade increased and became more profitable. Until about 1300, the number of people in Europe grew steadily larger. Prices of many goods rose because of scarcity.

town Guilds

Merchant and craft guilds were brotherhoods of people selling or making goods. Members promised to help one another and promote the wealth of their community. Merchant guilds protected local businesses and encouraged honesty. Craft guilds trained apprentices (learners) and encouraged high standards. There was one guild for each skill or "mastery." After about six or seven years, apprentices became journeymen (qualified workers). An experienced journeyman or journeywoman might submit his or her best work—a **"masterpiece"**—to craft masters. If they approved, he or she became a master as well.

▼ Craft **guilds** and brotherhoods of merchants paid for magnificent buildings in which to display their goods for sale. The Cloth Hall at Ieper (Ypres) in Flanders (now Belgium) was founded soon after 1300 and enlarged several times during the Middle Ages, as Flemish trading towns grew wealthier.

◄ These craftsmen are making and testing silver coins in fifteenth-century France. They are hammering finely detailed metal dies, which are stamps marked with the design of each coin onto thin, plain disks of metal called blanks. The master of the mint (coin-making workshop) examines a finished coin.

in coin, rather than receiving food, fuel, housing, or other benefits. The old system of **barter** used by early medieval communities was replaced by trade using mostly silver coins. Coins were issued by kings as a sign of their rank and power.

Coins were made by skilled craftspeople in royal or civic mints. The silver to make them came from mines in German and Czech lands. Because coins were made of precious metal, however, they were tempting targets for criminals. Thieves clipped (trimmed) shavings around each coin's edge. **Forgers** made imitations. To detect these deceptions, traders and market officials checked coinage by weight on balances or scales.

Certain coins, especially dinars from Muslim countries and florins from Florence in Italy, were respected for their high standard and accepted by traders in many lands. These coins were preferred at markets and fairs by money changers, who exchanged one country's coinage for another so that merchants could trade.

Florence was also a center of international banking, together with cities in what is now

There was a crisis around 1350, however, when the European population decreased by at least 40 percent because of the Black Death, or plague. In many places, survivors prospered economically. Since workers were suddenly in short supply, their wages rose, and they had money to spend.

After about 1300, most farmworkers—the majority of the medieval population—were paid

ENGLISH COINAGE, 1250

*"About this time, the English coin was so very badly **debased** by money-clippers and forgers that neither natives or foreigners could think about it without angry eyes or disturbed feelings. . ."* [19]

MONKS AT BURY SAINT EDMUNDS, ENGLAND, HAD TO BORROW, 1137

"Every monk . . . of his own free will . . . owed debts to Christians and Jews. Often the silk robes and gold chalice of the church were pledged [used as guarantee for loans], without the knowledge or agreement of the other monks." [20]

Germany. Traditionally, the Christian and Islamic religions banned lending at interest. The Jewish religion, however, placed few restrictions on lending money to Christians, so traders, rulers, city governments, and even the Church itself, often borrowed money from Jews.

As trade increased, businessmen needed ways of managing their money. International banks, such as the Bardi and the Perruzi in Italy and the Fuggers in Germany, became more important and powerful. They began to use new **Arabic numerals** and a new system (called double entry) of recording money spent and money owing. Long-distance traders also developed new ways of transferring wealth from one country to another. They no longer wanted to carry heavy, bulky coins that were hard to conceal and easy to steal. To help them, in the fourteenth century, banks began to issue "bills of exchange" (written promises by purchasers to pay money to sellers at a bank near their home). Banks also agreed to transfer money from one merchant's account to another as a way of settling debts. The first paper checks (written instructions to banks to pay money out of an account) appeared in Italy in about 1300.

Town Government

Rich or poor, all town dwellers had special legal status. Unlike many other medieval people, they were personally free. Only favored families,

▼ Bankers talk to their customers in fifteenth-century Italy, while bank clerks behind desks check payments and count out money. This picture was painted to decorate a list of tax payers in the city of Siena.

however, had full civic rights as citizens or "**burghers**." Only they could own property in a town, choose its government, and buy or sell goods without paying tolls and taxes.

By the end of the Middle Ages, many trading cities were governed by merchants or master craftsmen. They served on town councils and became mayors, **bailiffs**, and aldermen. They made local laws, appointed watchmen and police officers, and punished petty criminals, such as pickpockets, burglars, and cheats. They gave money to build town halls, churches, schools, and hospitals and to repair city gates and walls. They left money in their wills to feed and clothe poor people and to improve public health. They also agreed to business deals with each other and with other rich trading towns.

▲ Wealthy merchants played an important part in town government. They also contributed generously to charities, such as schools and hospitals. Like fifteenth-century Flemish townsman Jean de Witte, pictured here with his wife and a skull (to remind both of their eventual deaths), they commissioned fine portraits to hang in churches and gave money for prayers to help their souls reach heaven.

Some trading families took complete control of their local government and founded new ruling dynasties. The most powerful were in Italy, where merchants and businessmen—such as the Medici of Florence, who were bankers—ruled rich city-states. They paid for many splendid palaces, churches, paintings, and statues as signs of their family's prestige and power. Their success in business made them rich enough to hire private armies and challenge other European leaders.

traveling Beyond europe

eople in medieval Europe produced enough food to keep themselves alive and enough fabric and timber to clothe and house themselves. Nevertheless, they lacked the raw materials, secret skills, and advanced technology to produce expensive luxuries, such as silk and porcelain, that wealthy families liked to buy.

Goods from Far Places

Europe did not have the soils or climate to produce some valuable items, such as sugar to sweeten dishes, medicines to ease pain, and spices to add strong flavors to dull meals. It did not have rich deposits of precious stones, warm seas where oysters grew pearls, or tropical plants and animals used to make sweet, heavy scents. Since Roman times, however, there had been a long tradition of international trade. Exotic goods had been carried westward to Europe from Asia and the Far East. In medieval times, similar items were still on sale—at high prices—in European markets, shops, and showrooms.

A CAPTURED MUSLIM CARAVAN'S GOODS IN THE MIDDLE EAST, 1192

"Horses and camels . . . mules loaded with spices of different kinds and of great value, gold and silver, cloaks of silk, purple and scarlet robes . . . arms and weapons . . . coats of mail . . . costly cushions, pavilions [big, luxurious temporary shelters], tents, biscuits, bread, barley, grain, meal [flour] . . . conserves [fruit preserved in sugar] . . . medicines, basins . . . chess-boards, silver dishes and candlesticks, pepper, cinnamon, sugar, and wax . . . an immense sum of money." [21]

▼ These pottery bowls were made in western Asia about 1400. They are decorated with typical Islamic geometrical designs. Brightly-colored Asian pottery like this and more delicate Chinese porcelain were both highly-prized by medieval European buyers and sellers.

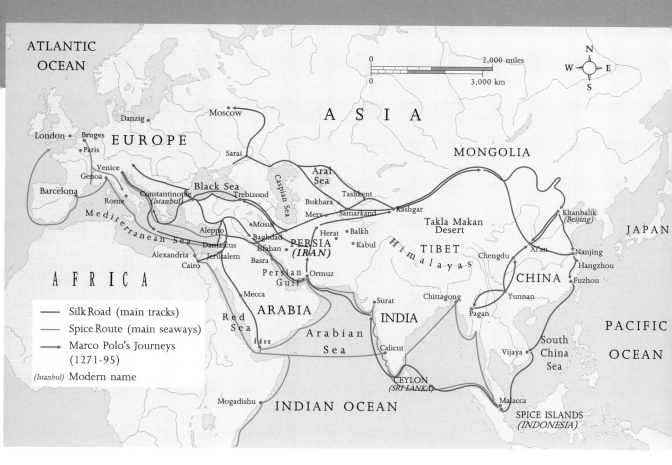

ATLANTIC OCEAN

A S I A

MONGOLIA

Moscow

London • Bruges • EUROPE
• Paris
Sarai

Venice
Genoa •
Barcelona

Rome
Constantinople
(Istanbul)

Black Sea
Trebizond

Aral
Sea

Tashkent

Kashgar

Khanbalik
(Beijing)

JAPAN

Mediterranean Sea

Aleppo
Damascus
Alexandria
Jerusalem
Cairo

Mosul
Baghdad
Isfahan
Basra

Herat • Balkh
• Kabul

PERSIA
(IRAN)

Caspian Sea

Bukhara
Merv • Samarkand

Takla Makan
Desert

H i m a l a y a s

TIBET

Chengdu

Xi'an

Nanjing
Hangzhou

CHINA • Fuzhou

A F R I C A

Persian
Gulf
Ormuz

Mecca

Red
Sea

ARABIA

Surat

Chittagong

Yunnan

Pagan

INDIA

Arabian
Sea

Calicut

Vijaya •

South
China
Sea

PACIFIC

OCEAN

Aden

CEYLON
(SRI LANKA)

Mogadishu • INDIAN OCEAN

Malacca

SPICE ISLANDS
(INDONESIA)

— Silk Road (main tracks)
— Spice Route (main seaways)
→ Marco Polo's Journeys (1271-95)
(Istanbul) Modern name

0 ____ 2,000 miles
0 ____ 3,000 km

N
W ✦ E
S

▲ Medieval merchants made their own travel arrangements. There were no fixed routes for them to follow. Many of them chose to travel along well-known networks of overland paths or along seaways that had been pioneered by other voyagers before them. Later historians have given these networks names that reflect the main goods traded by merchants traveling along them—the Silk Road and the Spice Route.

Silk Road, Spice Route

Medieval traders, like the Romans before them, followed two main trading routes to the East. One, known as the "Silk Road," was a network of tracks leading overland from the eastern shores of the Mediterranean, through Persia (now Iran) and central Asia to Mongolia and, finally, China. The other, a series of sea journeys known as the "Spice Route," ran from the Mediterranean through the Red Sea across the Indian Ocean to India and present-day Sri Lanka, then south to the **Spice Islands** (now part of Indonesia).

Both routes were very long and full of dangers. It might take more than a year to reach China from the Middle East. The Silk Road tracks ran through stony wastelands with no freshwater to

drink, over high snowy mountains, across vast, featureless **steppe** grassland, and through the fearsome Desert of Lop (Takla Makan), where travelers—it was said—were led away from their path across the constantly shifting sands by mirages, mysterious voices, and tricks played by evil **djinns** (spirits).

The Spice-Route voyage from the Red Sea also took many months. Travelers risked calms, storms, shipwrecks, sunstroke, starvation, and scurvy—a dangerous disease caused by lack of fresh fruit and vegetables. In ports, valuable cargos might be seized by corrupt officials or by local rulers hoping to make an extra profit.

Travelers along both routes had to rely on interpreters and local guides. With luck, they

would avoid local wars or outbreaks of deadly diseases, such as plague, cholera, and malaria.

In fact, few European merchants traveled all the way along either of these routes. On the Silk Road they usually completed the first few stages of the journey, from Constantinople in the Byzantine Empire or from Venice in Italy to international trading posts on the shores of the Black Sea. There they met Arab or Asian traders who had traveled east to the great market cities, such as Samarkand and Bukhara. Home of Uzbek and Tatar peoples, these rich cities were conquered in the thirteenth century by nomad Mongol warriors led by fierce warlike leaders, Genghis Khan (ruled 1206–1227) and Timur Lenk (Tamerlane who ruled 1369–1405). Merchants from China and Afghanistan traveled there to do business with merchants arriving from lands to the west.

Europeans trading along the Spice Route traveled to ports in Egypt or the Persian Gulf on the eastern coast of Africa. There, they met Arab traders who had sailed across the Indian Ocean to strike deals with merchants from India. The

Indian traders sold goods they had purchased from producers and brokers in lands farther south and east. Spice-Route travelers made use of regular monsoon winds from the southwest to travel faster to India and to make their voyages with greater certainty.

LETTER FROM GENGHIS KHAN TO A RULER IN WESTERN ASIA, 1218

"I am ruler of the lands of the rising sun while you rule those of the setting sun. Let us conclude a firm treaty of friendship and peace. Merchants and their caravans should come and go in both directions, carrying the valuable products and ordinary goods from my land to yours, just as they do from your land to mine." [21]

There were some exceptions to this general pattern, however. In the thirteenth century, when the Mongols ruled most of central Asia, it was safer than ever before to travel along the Silk Road. During this "Mongol Peace," several European merchants, explorers, and missionaries ventured eastward all the way to China. The most famous was Marco Polo, a member of a merchant family in Venice, Italy. Between 1271 and 1292, Polo traveled to China, then worked for Kublai Khan, the Mongol emperor, journeying through Asia to report on the Mongols' newly-conquered lands.

Soon after 1300, wars between rival Mongol leaders made it dangerous to travel along the Silk Road and threatened to **disrupt** east-west trade. Still, Asian goods, especially spices, remained very popular with Europeans, so merchants and explorers set out to discover a new way of bringing silks, spices, and other Asian produce into Europe.

European travelers on the Silk Road

1238–1240: Andrew of Longjumeau. French. Visits Mongols.

1245–1247: Giovanni de Plano Carpini. Italian. To Mongol ruler's court.

1253–1255: William of Rubruck. Flemish. To Mongols.

1255–1269: Maffeo Polo. Italian. To Russia, Bukhara, and China.

1291–1294: Giovanni de Montecorvino. Italian. To China, Persia, and India.

1316–1330: Orderic of Pordenone. Italian. To China, India, and Tibet.

1338–1353: Giovanni de Marignolli. Italian. To China.

1396–1402: Johann Schiltberger. German. Captured by Turks, then Mongols. To Russia, Georgia, Armenia, and Siberia.

▼ This fourteenth-century French illustration shows Italian traveler Marco Polo presenting a copy of the Gospels (part of the Bible) to Kublai Khan. It was a present from the pope, leader of the Roman Catholic Church, to the emperor. The pope hoped that European travelers would spread the Christian faith to distant lands.

Around Africa

In 1291, two Italians, Ugolino and Guido Vivaldi, set off from the port of Genoa in Italy. They aimed to sail around Africa to reach India, "which no European had ever attempted" and to bring home "goods profitable from there." The Vivaldis probably reached the Canary Islands and perhaps the coast of West Africa. After this they disappeared, but their voyage was not forgotten.

By 1400, memories of the Vivaldi voyage encouraged other Europeans to explore the seas around Africa as well as the African mainland. They hoped to trade in slaves and gold. Sailors were helped by Portugal's Prince Henry the Navigator (lived 1394 to 1460), who funded many voyages. In 1415, Portuguese troops captured the island of Ceuta off North Africa across the Strait of Gibraltar from Spain. In 1444, Genoese explorer Malfante crossed the Sahara Desert to reach the famous African city of Timbuktu (now Tombouctou, Mali). In 1471, Portugal set up a slave-trading station on the West African coast.

Trade and Exploration

In 1453, **Ottoman** Turks captured Constantinople and halted overland trade with Asia. Urgently,

Asian Produce Purchased by a Wealthy English Household, 1413

Three pounds of pepper
Two pounds of ginger
Two pounds of cinnamon
Two pounds of cloves
Forty pounds of almonds
Four pounds of rice
Six pounds of dates
Ten pounds of raisins
One pound of sugar [24]

merchants in Genoa—who relied on Asian trade—sponsored fresh attempts to reach India by sea. During 1487 to 1488, Portuguese sailors rounded the southern tip of Africa; in 1498, other Portuguese travelers arrived in India.

Portugal's rival and close neighbor, the powerful kingdom of Spain, also hoped to find a sea route to Asia's Spice Islands. In 1492, they paid for three small ships, captained by Christopher Columbus, to explore a new route for trading with Asia by sailing west across the Atlantic Ocean.

◄ The fort of El Mina, in Ghana, West Africa, was founded in 1482 by Portuguese explorers hoping to trade in gold. It soon became a center of slave trading, however, and African men, women, and children were shipped from Ghana to southern Europe and, later, South America and the Caribbean. After the end of the Middle Ages, El Mina fort was rebuilt. The strong walls in this photo date from 1637.

◀ A Portuguese merchant ship is pictured on a ceramic tile around 1498, at the end of the Middle Ages. Portuguese explorers who sailed along the coast of West Africa and around the Cape of Good Hope made long, daring ocean voyages in wind-powered ships like this one.

Columbus died believing he had reached Japan. Others, however, led by explorer Amerigo Vespucci, from Florence, Italy, realized Columbus had landed on a "new" or "unknown" continent. This astounding news challenged Europe's view of itself and its relations with other regions. It made Europeans question settled medieval ideas and what it meant to be a "civilized" human being. It ended old patterns of traveling and trading and introduced new opportunities, excitements, and dangers.

Like Henry the Navigator, and many other fifteenth-century voyagers, Columbus combined a wish to explore with a keen interest in making money through trade. His voyage achieved more than all earlier travelers. It revealed to medieval people just how little they knew about their world. Columbus's voyage showed that the Earth was much bigger than scholars had previously believed. It contained more land, different peoples, and wider oceans.

A VOYAGE TO THE CARIBBEAN IN 1494

"We spent twenty-nine days with terrible weather, bad food, and worse drink, but for the ardent [burning] desire for gold we all kept ourselves strong and daring."
Christopher Columbus [25]

▶ This map was made by pioneer German cartographer Martin Waldseemuller (1470–1518) in 1507, just after the end of the Middle Ages. It was one of the very first to show the world with four continents: Europe, Africa, Asia, and America. Australia, New Zealand, the Arctic, and Antarctic are still not shown. They would not be known to European travelers and traders for another one hundred years or more.

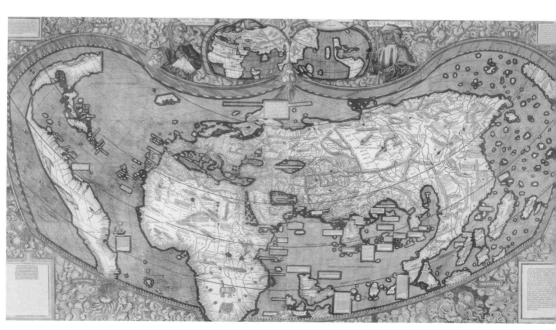

330
The Roman Empire divides. Constantinople (now Istanbul) becomes capital of the Byzantine Empire.

476
The last Roman emperor leaves Rome

c. 600-700
New trading towns are set up on both sides of the North Sea.

711
Muslims, mostly from northern Africa, take control of southern Spain.

794
Charlemagne, king of the Franks, reforms coins, weights, and measures throughout his empire to encourage trade.

849-899
King Alfred the Great of Wessex, England, builds burghs (fortified towns) to defend his kingdom. Traders come to live in them.

885-886
Vikings attack Paris, in France.

895-896
Magyars from Central Asia arrive in Hungary.

900-1100
Rus (Vikings living in Russia) trade with the Byzantine Empire. They travel overland and along rivers to the Black Sea.

c. 1075-1122
Italian towns win rights to govern themselves.

1096
First Crusaders leave Europe to fight in the Holy Land.

c. 1100-1300
The Church builds hospitals in towns; town councils make laws to improve cleanliness and public health.

c. 1175-1250
This is the great age of international trade fairs in the Champagne region of France.

1204
From this date until the end of the Middle Ages, Venice, Italy, controls shipping and trade in the Mediterranean Sea.

1206
The Mongol empire grows powerful. "Mongol Peace" encourages east-west overland trade.

1241
The Hanseatic League of trading cities and towns is founded.

1245-1247
Giovanni de Plano Carpini visits Mongol emperor's court and writes about it.

1252
The rich Italian city of Florence makes first gold coins for almost five hundred years— a sign that trade is flourishing.

1265
Representatives of boroughs (towns) become members of English parliament.

1271-1295
Marco Polo travels in China and Asia.

1277
Genoa, Italy, sets up regular sea-trading route between Mediterranean and North Sea.

1291
Vivaldi brothers set off from Genoa to try to sail around southern tip of Africa.

1325
Orderic of Pordenone, Italy, reaches Tibet.

c. 1340
About fifteen cities in Europe have more than fifty thousand inhabitants.

1347-1351
The Black Death kills at least 40 percent of Europe's population resulting in a temporary collapse of trade.

1444
Italian explorer Malfante reaches Tombouctou (Timbuktu).

1453
Constantinople is conquered by Muslim Ottoman Turks.

1471
The Portuguese set up slave-trading post on the coast of West Africa.

1487-1488
Portuguese ships sail around the southern tip of Africa.

1492
Christopher Columbus sails across the Atlantic Ocean.

Source References:

1. C. Warren Hollister. *Medieval Europe: A Short History,* Wiley, 1964, p. 1.

2. Adapted from J. Jacobs, *Jewish Contributions to Civilization*, Jewish Publication Society of America, 1919, p. 194.

3. Ralph of Coggeshall. Adapted from: D. Danziger and J. Gillingham, *1215—The Year of Magna Carta*, Hodder and Stoughton, 2003, p. 270.

4. A medieval writer. From Jordanes, *The Origin and Deeds of the Goths,* translated by Charles C. Mierow, quoted in web site: www.ucalgary.ca/~vandersp/Courses/texts/jordget.html

5. Quoted in D. Danziger and J. Gillingham, *see above*, p. 290.

6. Richer of Reims, a French monk. Adapted and simplified by author, translated by Michael Markowski from R. Latouche (ed.), *Histoire of France*, Paris, 1964, vol. 2, pp. 225-230.

7. King Edward I to the citizens of Dunstable. Quoted in D. Danziger and J. Gillingham, *see above*, p. 49.

8. Quoted in C. Culpin, *Medieval Realms*, Collins Educational, 1991, p. 19.

9. Richer of Reims, a French monk, *see above*, p. 225-230.

10. Reprinted in R. C. Cave and H. H. Coulson, *A Source Book for Medieval Economic History*, The Bruce Publishing Co., 1936; reprinted Biblo and Tannen, 1965, p. 153.

11. Walter Map, an eyewitness. C. Culpin, *see above*, p. 15.

12. Walter Bower. D Hall, *Burgess, Merchant and Priest,* Birlinn, 2002, p. 41.

13. Pope Urban II. Quoted in J. Riley-Smith, *Atlas of the Crusades*, Times Books, 1991, p. 26.

14. A monk eyewitness. From the *Annals of St. Bertin*, quoted in Internet Medieval Sourcebook, source: www.fordham.edu/halsall/source/834bertin.html

15. R. McKitterick (ed.) *Mapping History: Medieval World*, Times Books, 2003, p. 100.

16. Adapted from: Matthew of Paris, *English History*, trans. J.A. Giles, 1852, Vol. I, p. 410; reprinted in R. C. Cave & H. H. Coulson, *see above*, pp. 107-108.

17. Reprinted in R. C. Cave & H. H. Coulson, *see above*, p. 302.

18. Summarized by author from C. Culpin, *see above*, p. 40.

19. Adapted from Matthew of Paris, *see above*, p. 262.

20. Adapted from *Chronicle of Jocelin de Brakelond*, reprinted in Internet Medieval Sourcebook: www.fordham.edu/halsall/source/1173badloans.html

21. Adapted from Geoffrey of Vinsauf, *Itinerary of Richard I and others to the Holy Land*, translated in *Chronicles of the Crusades*, ed. H. G. Bohn, 1848, p. 307, reprinted in R. C. Cave and H. H. Coulson, *see above*, p. 155.

22. Quoted in J. Tucker, *The Silk Road, Art and History*, Philip Wilson Publishers, 2003, p. 220.

23. Christopher Columbus. W. D. Phillips, Jr. and C. Rahn Phillips, *The Worlds of Christopher Columbus*, Cambridge University Press, 1992, p. 204.

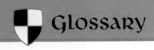

amber   Fossilized tree resin, used to make jewelry

Arabic numerals   The figures (1, 2, 3, etc.) used today. Invented in India, they were introduced to medieval Europe by Muslim travelers.

bailiffs   Officials who collected money

Baltic region   Area around the Baltic Sea in northern Europe. Today this includes Finland, Estonia, Latvia, Lithuania, and Poland.

barbarian   An ancient Greek word, used by Romans and later Europeans to describe foreigners. It suggests that foreigners are wild, brutal, and savage.

barter   Exchange goods for others of equal or similar value

beacons   Fires used to send signals

burghers   Citizens with rights to live and trade in a town and elect the town government

Byzantine Empire   The area in eastern Europe around ancient Byzantium (now Istanbul, Turkey). At various times between 628–1143, Byzantine emperors ruled lands now known as Turkey, Cyprus, Greece, Albania, Croatia, Iraq, Syria, southern Italy, and areas of the North African coast.

canvas   Strong, thick cloth

caravans   Travelers who group together to help each other, usually in a hostile region, such as a desert

cartographer   A person who makes maps

cattle drovers   People who led herds of cattle to market to sell

Celtic   Belonging to a civilization that was strong in many parts of Europe from about 800 B.C. to A.D. 100. The Celts were famous fighters and craftspeople.

chemise   Loose smock made of thin fabric, worn under outer clothes

Crusades   Wars fought between Christians and Muslims, pagans, or heretics

debased   Damaged, reduced in value, and no longer trusted

disrupt   To stop, delay, or disorganize

dissidents   People who disagree with the teachings of a religion

djinn   Arabic word meaning bad or angry spirit

forgers   People who make imitation items, intending to deceive

Franks   A nomadic people who settled in France from about A.D. 500

graze   To lead animals, such as cows, sheep, or cattle to grass, which they eat as food

guilds   Associations of people working at the same occupation or craft

inaccessible   Something that is hard or impossible to reach

lateen   Triangular sails originally used by ships in the Mediterranean Sea

masterpiece   An example of fine work

medieval   A word that relates to and describes the Middle Ages

mule   An animal used for carrying loads, bred from a horse mated with a donkey

Orthodox Churches   A branch of the Christian Church led by the patriarch (senior bishop) of Constantinople with allied Churches in Russia and the Balkans

Ottoman   Belonging to a Turkish ruling dynasty, founded by Othman I (ruled 1299–1326)

packhorses   Horses that carried heavy loads

pagan   A word used by medieval Christians and Muslims to describe people who did not share their religious beliefs

parliaments   Conferences to discuss public affairs, or the organization of political groups to form a government

pilgrimage   A religious journey to a holy place

pillory   Wooden frame in which criminals were locked while people threw rubbish, sticks, and stones at them

pilots   (at sea) Sailors with expert local knowledge who help steer ships into harbors

pitch   Sticky black tar, used to cover large items and make them waterproof

portolans   Written descriptions of the coast, sometimes with simple diagrams of compass directions. Used to help navigate at sea.

progresses   Ceremonial journeys made by kings or queens to various areas in their domain

prow   The front end of a ship

quicksand   Loose, wet sand that traps—and eventually drowns—anyone walking across it

relics   Physical remains of a holy or important person

Roman Empire   The people and lands that belonged to ancient Rome, consisting of most of southern Europe and northern Africa from Britain to the Middle East

shafts   Long wooden poles fixed to the front of a cart. Horses were harnessed to them, to pull the cart along.

shutters   Wooden boards fixed across windows to keep out wind, rain, and light

Spice Islands   Southeast Asian islands, now part of Indonesia, where cloves, nutmeg, and other spices grow

squire   Young man training to be a knight; a knight's assistant

steppe   Dry, open, level grassland

stern   The back end of a ship

tapestries   Large woven pictures, usually hung on walls

tolls   Taxes paid for the right to pass along a road, cross a bridge, or enter and trade in a town

wreckers   People on shore who lured ships toward dangerous coasts, hoping to steal goods on board

further Information

Books:

Elliott, Lynne. *Medieval Towns, Trade, and Travel*. New York: Crabtree Publishing Company, 2004.

Hinds, Kathryn. *The City* (Life in the Middle Ages). New York: Benchmark Books, 2000.

Langley, Andrew. *Medieval Life* (Eyewitness Books). New York: DK Publishing, 2004.

Macdonald, Fiona. *Women in Medieval Times* (The Other Half of History). Chicago: Peter Bedrick Books, 2000.

Web Sites:

An Internet Medieval Sourcebook
www.fordham.edu/halsall/sbook.html
This medieval history sourcebook has copies and translations of many medieval texts, plus useful links.

Paul J. Gans's Web Pages
scholar.chem.nyu.edu
This site features a time line and information on many developments in technology during the Middle Ages. Search through the Subject Index, then click on topic of interest.

The Middle Ages
www.learner.org/exhibits/middleages.html
Created for the Annenberg Foundation and the Corporation for Public Broadcasting, this site has information on various medieval topics.

Medieval Art
www.metmuseum.org/home.asp
The Metropolitan Museum of Art web site. To find medieval art, first click on "Timeline of Art History" on home page, then "Years 500–1000" or "Years 1000–1400," then area of world, e.g., Europe, then region of Europe icon, then icon of dynasty or empire desired. There is also a detailed time line for each region.

Videos/DVDs

Just the Facts: The Middle Ages. Goldhil Home Media, 2001. (VHS)

Life in the Middle Ages: The Merchant. Schlessinger Media, 2002. (VHS)

Index

Africa, 12, 40, 42, 43
Alps, 6, 7, 28
Arles (France), 22
armies, 9, 26–27, 33, 37
Asian pottery, 38
astrolabes, 22

bailiffs, 37
Balkans, 6
Baltic region, 28
bandits, 19, 20
banking, 5, 34–36
barter, 35
bazaars, 40
bills of exchange, 36
Black Death, 35
Bologna (Italy), 24, 30
Bukhara, 40, 41
burghers, 36–37
Bury Saint Edmunds
  (England), 36
Byzantine Empire, 28, 40

Canterbury cathedral
  (England), 25
caravans, 4, 16, 38, 40
caravansaries, 20
Carpathians, 6
carriages, 16
cartographers, 12, 43
carts, 14, 16, 17, 24, 27
Catholic Church, 9
cattle drovers, 24
Ceuta (North Africa), 42
Champagne region (France),
  32
Charlemagne, king of the
  Franks, 17, 23, 28
Christian Church, 4, 5, 8, 30,
  35
Christianity, 4, 8, 9, 24–25,
  31, 41
churches, 8, 21, 37
cities, trading, 28, 32, 37
climate, 6, 10–11, 38
Cloth Hall (Ieper, Flanders),
  34
coinage, 28, 35–36
Cologne (Köln, Germany), 28,
  33
Columbus, Christopher, 42–43
craft guilds, 34
criminals, 16, 19, 24, 35, 37
Crusades, 5, 27

dangers of travel, 10–11, 14,
  19–21, 28, 39
Danube River, 6, 23
Desert of Lop (Takla Makan),
  39
disease, 4, 10, 32, 35, 39, 40
djinns, 39
Dublin, Ireland, 7, 32

education, 4
El Mina (Ghana, West Africa), 42
Europe, 4, 6–9, 10, 11, 12,
  17, 20–24, 27, 28, 30, 32,
  33, 35, 37, 38, 42, 43
  contacts and conflicts in, 9
  divided peoples of, 8–9
  geographical features of, 6
  travel in, 10

exotic goods, 38
exploration, 42–43

Faeroe Islands, 6
fairs, 4, 24, 30, 31–32, 35
faith journeys, 24–25, 27
farming, 4, 6, 18, 19, 24, 27,
  35
fishing, 6, 19, 21, 24
flooding, 11, 17
Florence (Italy), 35, 37, 43
food, 4, 5, 6, 7, 14, 19, 20, 27,
  28, 30, 32, 35, 38
foot travel, 6, 14, 16–17, 27
forgers, 35
Fuggers bank, 36

galleys, 28–29
Genghis Khan, 40
Genoa (Italy), 28, 42
geography, 6, 12
goods, 20, 21, 28, 30, 31, 32,
  33, 34, 37, 38, 39, 41, 42
government, 4–5, 17, 19, 32,
  36–37
government travel, 24
grazing, 32
guides, 14, 39
guilds, 34

hackneys, 16
Hamburg (Germany), 33
Hanseatic League, 32, 33
Henry the Navigator, prince of
  Portugal, 42, 43
heretics, 9
holidays, 31–32
Holy Land, 27
horse, travel by, 13, 14–17,
  20, 27
housing, 19, 23, 33–34, 35,
  38

Indian Ocean, 22, 39, 40
inland waterways, 23
international banks, 36
islands, 6, 12, 21, 39, 42

John, king of England, 10, 21
Judaism, 9, 35–36

knights, 14, 27
Kublai Khan, 5, 41

lakes, 14, 23
languages, 6, 8, 9
lateen sails, 22
legal systems, 8, 37
litters, 16
local travel, 24

Makkah (Mecca, Arabia), 25
Malfante, 42
maps, 11–12, 14, 43
Marignolli, Giovanni de, 41
markets, 4, 19, 24, 30–32, 35,
  38, 40
Marseilles (France), 28
masterpieces, 34
mayors, 37
Medici family, 37
merchant guilds, 34
merchant "princes," 32

merchants, 4, 5, 9, 19, 20, 23,
  24, 28, 30–34, 36, 37, 39,
  40, 41, 42
migrants, 19, 27
missionaries, 8, 24, 41
moneylending, 35–36
Mongol Peace, 41
Mongols, 5, 40, 41
monks, 6, 20, 24, 36
Mont Blanc, 7
Montecorvino, Giovanni de, 41
mountains, 6, 7, 12, 16, 17,
  24, 39
Muslims, 9, 18, 20, 22, 25,
  27, 31, 35, 38

Naples (Italy), 24, 28–29
navigation, 12, 21, 22
nobles, 14, 16, 17, 24

Orderic of Pordenone, 41
Orthodox Churches, 9
Ottoman Turks, 42

packhorses, 10, 16, 17, 18,
  20, 24, 27
pagans, 8, 24
palfreys, 14
Paris (France), 24, 27, 28, 32
parliaments, 5, 24
Perruzi bank, 36
pilgrimages, 11, 24–25, 27
pilots, 10, 14, 22
plague, 35, 40
pollution, 32
Polo, Marco, 5, 41
Polo, Maffeo, 5, 41
poor, 5, 14, 32, 36, 37
population, 4, 5, 35
portolans, 21, 22
Prague (Czech Republic), 28
prow, 21
Pyrenees, 6

relics, 10, 25
religion, 4, 8, 9, 35
Rhine River, 6, 23, 28
Rhone River, 6
rivers, 6, 11, 12, 14, 17, 18,
  21, 23, 28, 32
roads, 5, 12, 14, 17–19, 34
Roman Empire, 4, 5, 8, 38
Roman roads, 17–18

sailing ships, 21–22, 43
sailors, 10, 22, 42
Saint Andrew's Shrine
  (Scotland), 25
Saint Bartholomew's fair
  (London), 32
Saint Bernard, 6
Saint Ives fair (England), 32
Saint James, 25
Salisbury market (England), 32
Samarkand, 40
Santiago (Saint James) de
  Compostela (Spain), 25
Schiltberger, Johann, 41
scurvy, 39
sea monsters, 10
seas, 6, 7, 10, 14, 19, 21–23,
  27, 28, 38, 42
sea travel, 21–22, 39

servants, 16, 19, 21
settlers, 27
ships, 6, 14, 21–23, 24, 27,
  28-29, 33, 42, 43
shutters, 33
Silk Road, 39–41
slavery, 30–31, 42
Spice Islands, 39, 42
Spice Route, 39–41
squires, 14, 16
staffs/staves, 14
stave church (Urnes, Norway), 8
steppe, 39
stern, 21, 22

Takla Makan Desert, 39
tapestries, 28
taxes, 7, 17, 32, 37
Timbuktu (Tombouctou, Mali),
  42
Timgad (Algeria), 18
Timur Lenk (Tamerlane), 40
town councils, 19, 37
towns, 4, 5, 17, 19, 20, 24,
  27, 32
  governments of, 36–37
  living in, 32–34
  markets in, 19, 30–32
  trading towns, 18, 32, 34, 37
trade, 4, 5, 9, 28, 38, 41
  coinage and banking, 34–36
  and exploration, 42–43
  markets for, 30–32
  town governments, 36–37
  and town living, 32–34
  travel for, 27–29
trade goods, 28, 30
trade routes, 24, 27–28, 39–41
travel, 5, 9, 10–23
  around Africa, 42
  beyond Europe, 38–43
  dangers of, 10–11, 14,
    19–21, 28, 39
  for faith, 24–25, 27
  by foot or horseback, 6, 13,
    14–17, 20, 27
  for government, 24
  local, 24
  maps and guides, 11, 12, 14
  by migrants and settlers, 27
  places to stay during, 20–21
  roads, 5, 12, 14, 17–19
  speed of, 17, 21
  for trade, 24, 27–29
  for war, 26–27
  by water, 10, 14, 21–23
travelers' tales, 14
*Travels of Sir John Mandeville,
  The*, 4

universities, 4, 5, 24

Venice (Italy), 5, 23, 28, 40, 41
Vespucci, Amerigo, 43
Vikings, 21, 27, 28
Vivaldi, Ugolino and Guido, 4?

wagons, 14, 17
Waldseemuller, Martin, 43
wars, 4, 5, 9, 26–27, 40, 41
water travel, 10, 14, 21–23
William of Rubruck, 41
wreckers, 21